Shapes

I See Squares

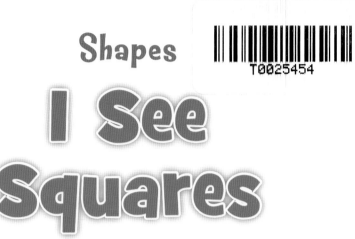

By Czeena Devera

 This square is green.

This square is **red**.

 This square is orange.

This square is blue.

 This square is yellow.

This square is **purple.**

8 This square is **pink**.

This square is **brown**.

 This square is white.

This square is **black.**

This square is gray.

This square is **colorful**.

square	yellow	black
green	purple	gray
red	pink	colorful
orange	brown	
blue	white	

Hello!
I'm yellow.

This square is green.
This square is red.
This square is orange.
This square is blue.
This square is yellow.
This square is purple.
This square is pink.
This square is brown.
This square is white.
This square is black.
This square is gray.
This square is colorful.

CHERRY BLOSSOM PRESS

Published in the United States of America by Cherry Lake Publishing Group
Ann Arbor, Michigan
www.cherrylakepublishing.com

Photo Credits: © bogdandimages/Shutterstock.com, front cover, 1; © Viktor1/Shutterstock.com, 2; © Gjermund/Shutterstock.com, 3; © P Maxwell Photography/Shutterstock.com, 4; © Atstock Productions/Shutterstock.com, 5; © Ariyaporn chumkong/Shutterstock.com, 6, 14; © Viktor Buzuyevskiy/Shutterstock.com, 7, back cover; © Savanevich Viktar/Shutterstock.com, 8; © MaraZe/Shutterstock.com, 9; © vanilla22/Shutterstock.com, 10; © darksoul72/Shutterstock.com, 11; © Pataradon Luangtongkum/Shutterstock.com, 12; © Pykodelbi/Shutterstock.com, 13

Copyright © 2021 by Cherry Lake Publishing Group
All rights reserved. No part of this book may be reproduced or utilized in any form or by any means without written permission from the publisher.

Cherry Blossom Press is an imprint of Cherry Lake Publishing Group.

Library of Congress Cataloging-in-Publication Data

Names: Devera, Czeena, author.
Title: I see squares / Czeena Devera.
Description: Ann Arbor, Michigan : Cherry Lake Publishing, 2021. | Series: Shapes | Audience: Grades K-1 | Summary: "Spot squares and identify colors in this book. Beginning readers will gain confidence with the Whole Language approach to literacy, a combination of sight words and repetition. Bold, colorful photographs correlate directly to the text to help guide readers as they engage with the book"— Provided by publisher.
Identifiers: LCCN 2020030242 (print) | LCCN 2020030243 (ebook) | ISBN 9781534179837 (paperback) | ISBN 9781534180840 (pdf) | ISBN 9781534182554 (ebook)
Subjects: LCSH: Square—Juvenile literature.
Classification: LCC QA482 .D484 2021 (print) | LCC QA482 (ebook) | DDC 516/.154—dc23
LC record available at https://lccn.loc.gov/2020030242
LC ebook record available at https://lccn.loc.gov/2020030243

Cherry Lake Publishing Group would like to acknowledge the work of the Partnership for 21st Century Learning, a Network of Battelle for Kids. Please visit *http://www.battelleforkids.org/networks/p21* for more information.

Printed in the United States of America
Corporate Graphics